WHERE POEMS ARE BORN

A Different Kind Of Poetry
by David D Jerald

God may be our father ….

But our mother is the fire …

D.D. Jerald

I was Born November 20th in the State of Washington, USA on the banks of the Snake river. My Dad was in the Military and I grew up in South Carolina, North Carolina, Mississippi, Washington, Oregon, California, and Arizona. I learned good things and bad things traveling from one place to the next. Making friends was a hard thing because it hurt when you left them behind. I learned to read the heck out of a road map. I loved military history, poetry, and Maps. I worked in a cement plant for 30 years before retiring. I now live in Hawaii.

The poets that I like the most are Sara Teasdale, Alfred Lord Tennyson and Ella Wheeler Wilcox and a lot more.

Welcome to 35 years of my poetry. I hope you enjoy.

CONTENTS

Poem 01

sa·gua·ro /sə'(g)wärō/
noun plural noun: saguaros

Saguaros

On a two lane highway..
Winding through the night.
Past countless tall Saguaros ..
Bathing in the full moonlight.

Through the midst of giants ..
All around me.. everywhere.
Saguaros .. arms held high ..
In silent wonder there.

Born on top a tall saguaro ..
And only in the dark of night.
Starlight gently washes them ..
Bold flowers Lily-white.

Saguaros, like an army frozen.
Waiting for the trumpets call.
Countless legions in green ..
Praying for the rain to fall.

Saguaro (Carnegiea gigantea) is a big tree-like cactus in the Sonoran Desert in southwestern Arizona. Night-blooming flowers appear around April. The saguaro blossom is the state flower of Arizona.

Poem 02

Inspired by a little girls
love for a Father who left
her and her mother.

A Childs Love

A child's love will never lie.
Or ever say my heart forgot.
Always there will never die ..
In times deserved ..In times when not.

A child's love is blind to wrong ..
And never can be bought.
Always there this love so strong ..
In times deserved .. In times when not.

I saw this kind of love up front and close. It
made my heart Ache.
and from that aching heart .. is where this poem
was   born.

Poem .. 03

Someone Somewhere

Is there someone somewhere meant for me?
Someone I'll never know.
One lonely heart .. waiting just for me ..
Somewhere I'll never go?
If someone somewhere is pointing at ..
The same old star that I can see.
Is someone somewhere in the night ..
All alone .. just like me.

Is someone somewhere reaching out ..
Somewhere I'll never go?
Someone I passed along the way ..
Someone I'll never know?
If someone somewhere is listening ..
To the same old song as I .. Could it be?
That someone somewhere is dancing ..
All alone .. just like me.

Have you ever felt .. Alone.
Well .. then you know from where this poem
was   born.

Poem 04

Where The Plains Touch The Sky

In her hair was an eagle feather ..
It was dancing in the wind.
She was riding straight and hard ..
To anywhere she'd never been.
She even closed her eyes and
Wished that pony could fly.
And I heard her laughing as she faded ..
Riding hard ..
To where the plains touch the sky.

She rode hard and fast to get away.
Away from what I'll never know.
But with eyes a closed and heart a fire ..
I wished that I could go.
With long hair flying she flew by.
And I heard her laughing as she faded ..
Riding hard ..
To where the plains touch the sky.

Did you ever want to just get away? Far away?

Poem .. 05

Never Lie

I like the way you dance so close.
My face against your hair.
I like the way your head lays ..
So softly .. on my shoulder there.

I like the way you gently smile.
As I pull you closer now to me.
And how you look into my eyes ..
Just to see what you can see.

I like the way so tenderly you kiss.
The way you cling to me so tight.
And oh .. the taste of you and how ..
You madly love me through the night.

I like your hush don't ever say
I love you .. for then true love will die.
And in my ear you softly whisper ..
Just say you promise .. I will never lie.

Is this asking so much? If you can't say .. you
love me .. ok .. just please.. never lie to me.

Poem .. 06

The Search

In my search for truth
I found it there at wounded knee.
I had to clinch my fist to calm
The rage inside of me.

In my search for God in heaven.
I banged upon his pearly door.
The Devil opened up and said to me ..
God ain't here no more.

In my search for peace I found it
Toe to toe with war.
And rushing into battle
I found myself in hell .. a place
I wasn't searching for.

In my search for strength
I found the flame that burns inside.
Which I turned into a raging fire ..
To protect my heart ..
And burn the word goodbye.

In my search for love
I found a place of sadness ..

And I thought of thee.
It was a place of broken vows
Where pieces of .. were scattered ..
As far as I could see.

Have you ever wanted to just beat the crap out of
..stomp it into the ground and burn the word
goodbye?

I   hate   that   word.

Poem .. 07

True Loves Light

In the dark alone
I searched for true loves light.
Oh damn that love so elusive ..
Just once to hold it tight.

So forward on I whispered said.
For true loves light
Just might be shinning ..
Yonder up ahead.

Are you still looking for true love? Who knows
.. it may still be out there waiting for you .. or
maybe you once found it long ago but were
stupid .. and tossed it away like a empty coke
can.

Poem .. 08

Rain

I remember the night the demons came
The rain was pouring down and I recall.
The pain inside me then I feel again ..
Every time the rains fall.

A little lie a cruel goodbye
Buried deep inside my brain.
A thought so sad I thought forgotten ..
Haunts me in the rain.

Those demons deep inside ..
Those unforgiving little pains.
The ones I thought I'm tougher than
But I'm not .. and then it rains.

Oh father sun .. oh mother moon
Stay bright outside my window pane.
For quietly inside of me the demons wait ..
So patiently for rain.

I suffered a broken heart many years ago all
while standing in the cold pouring rain.
I always think of that time .. every time it rains.

Poem .. 09

Trophies

Heads of beast .. trophies of the kill
There in eerie silence .. hanging on the wall.
If I killed for sport to test my skill
I'd hang up there some human heads ..
Or I'd hang no heads at all.

I know you hunters might be upset with me but I never could get used to seeing animal heads stuffed and mounted on a wall. Hence this poem was born .. with a little humor. Its just the way I roll.

Poem .. 10

Mother

I dreamed ..
Mother slammed her fist!
And the Stars blinked on.
Say it's not true she doesn't exist.
Or say it happened just because.
But in the darkest part of nothing
She asked for light and so there was.

Mother slammed her fist!
And by glory the sun turned on.
It's ungodly not true you insist.
It never happened that way!
But I saw the sun and her fire
Conquer the dark and free the day.

Mother slammed her fist!
And the Earth was born.
Say no way .. but she gave it a twist
And spun it around the Sun to stay.
A diamond adrift in a ocean of rocks ..
With only the moon to play.

Mother slammed her fist!

And dinosaurs were born.
God is a he .. not a she .. you insist
And It never happened that way.
Oh ye of little faith .. I saw them
Rulers of the night and the day.

In a Mother thrown fiery display
Mother slammed her fist!
And the dinosaurs were gone.
What thought forever ceased to exist.
But she left there the bones and a note ..
Death is but a breath .. and a whisper away.

Mother slammed her fist!
And humans were born.
Put my name on a long black list
For saying it happen that way.
But I saw humans full of hate
Killing each other, to her dismay.

Mother slammed her fist!
The Earth stopped and she jumped on.
Just the Devil enraged you insist.
Stake me and burn me for all that I say.
But I saw Mother chasing man
All through the night and the day.

Mother slammed her fist!
And the world went black.
Mother slammed her fist!
And the light came back.
Man blinked whimpered and said
Mother forgive me .. I was wrong.
Mother said .. No ..
You have been here way to long.

Mother slammed her fist!
And the world went black.
Jump up and down get mad .. I insist.
Try to explain it .. shouldn't take long.
But here in the dark and the nothing
The lights are out and the fires gone.

In the dark a fist slammed.
And a voice cried .. Light.
And by fire the dark was dammed.
The sun lit up and the stars blinked on.
I saw Mother .. the Earth .. and the Moon.
But man was gone.

I always wondered .. what if God was a woman.

Poem .. 11

Damned

I can hide away in the darkest of night.
To escape my sins so ashamed in the light.
But I am damned in the dark .. damned if I'm
not.
I can whimper I'm sorry so sorry I cry.
But I'm damned if I'm sorry .. a little or a lot.

I can hide neath a rock or crawl in a hole
To escape my guilt burning deep in my soul.
But I am damned if I do and damned if I won't.
I can pray to God .. lay me down to die.
But I am damned if I die and damned if don't.

Did you ever do something once in your life ..
that haunts you every day? .. and probably will
until   death?

Poem .. 12

The Seventh Day

God was bored the seventh Day.
So he challenged the Devil to play.
To a game of souls till one has all ..
Till Demons burn or Angles fall.

My version of what may have happened on the
7th day of creation. Ever read the King James
version of the bible? Geneses at least.

Poem .. 13

Burning Bright

Thank you for the Sun.
Who gives us warmth and light.
Of which there would be none
If deep inside there never was ..
Your fire burning bright.

Thank you for the Stars
Who guide us through the night.
The stars who couldn't shine
If far out there .. there never was ..
Your fire burning bright.

Thank you for the ones
Who love us wrong or right.
Who'd die for us .. but never would ..
If deep inside there never was
Your fire burning bright.

Thank you for the strength
To never fear in times I might.
To still this heart I never could
If deep inside there never was ..
Your fire burning bright.

Thank you for this Gift
The flame inside .. the purest of all light.
The spark of life I'd never have
If way out there .. there never was
Your fire burning bright.

Who ever your God may be .. who ever you see
as your creator .. he or she .. is the fire burning
bright   inside   your   heart.

Poem .. 14

Sheep in Armor

Eyes bulging .. dam it .. let me go
Tapping twitching there .. I said.
Sheep in armor crying
Going nowhere
Cause the light burned red.

In front behind and all around ..
A million more just like me.
All alive just barely dead.
Sheep in armor crying
Going nowhere ..
Cause the light burned red.

I was neck deep in traffic in Tucson Arizona .. it was 105 Degree's and we were all stopped by a red light. As I looked around this poem was born.

Poem .. 15

Fire

There burns the fire deep in every sun.
Burning there till the fires done.
The strength in starlight faraway
Fire blazing .. lighting up the milky way.

There burns the truth it will not hide.
In our hearts the flame that burns inside ..
Flickering meek as candlelight
Or blazing burning bright.

Fire flying burning through the sky
The kind we wish upon and why.
These humble words it does inspire ..
God may be our father ..
But our mother is the fire.

I believe in all kinds of Fire .. but I really believe
.. we were all born from Fire. Our Mother is the
fire.

Poem .. 16

Taps The last Goodbye

For the soldiers who marched away.
For the Mothers who watched them go.
Over row after row of white stones ..
Our sons and daughters there below.
For the fallen and the never conquered ..
The innocent slaughtered and the Buffalo.

For the ones who kept their word.
A promise .. for as long as the winds blow.
For freedom won and for freedom lost.
Over the dead I ask .. who is last to cry?
Just Listen .. hear the echo's dying ..
The bugler blowing taps .. the last goodbye.

A lone man blowing a haunting notes on a bugle
.. when a soldier is buried. If you have heard it
while someone you loved or respected greatly is
being buried .. you know what it sounds like. It
makes for one gut wrenching goodbye.

Poem .. 17

The Thrill of The Chase

I have stolen love with just a kiss.
Whispering for always in her embrace.
I've lied I'm in love when the truth was this ..
I lived for the thrill of the Chase.

I've killed in the shadow of the waving flag.
I've wallowed in blood in a far off place.
I did it for God and for country .. I'd brag.
I lied .. I lived for the thrill of the Chase.

I accept the truth I'll be dying alone.
Just me and death someday face to face.
And then off I'll run into the dark unknown ..
Like a howling dog .. to the thrill of the Chase.

In one way or another .. we all have done some
chasing   in   our   lives   ..   Right?

Poem .. 18

If I'd Been God that Day
When they burned young Joan of Arc
It was fire for truth .. she'd not betray.
Oh holy warrior .. brightest light in all the dark.
Fire wouldn't burn ..
If I'd been God that Day.

When they danced the ghost dance long ago.
Only silence echoed back from faraway.
I'd of sent a thundering herd of endless buffalo.
And bullets couldn't fly ..
If I'd been God that Day.

When Spartans died there at Thermopylae.
To the death there code they did obey.
Forever all 300 would guard my gates for me.
In full regalia shining bright ..
If I'd been God that Day.

When God found Adam hiding with Eve.
From the garden in sin he sent away.
I'd of forgiven them for being so naïve.
Then I'd of killed the snake ..
If I'd been God that Day.

I love reading military history … there were
many times I wished for the power to change it.

Poem .. 19

On Wings of Light

Here my love reach high up there and touch a
star.
Gaze in wonder at the fires blazing there .. so
far.
Witness how my love .. the magic in the
shinning light ..
Speeds you on your way from here .. into the
starry night.

Fly away my love .. on wings of light into the
sky.
Straight up into the heavens there .. to wonder
why.
And every time you go and gaze into the fires
light ..
I will wait for you .. right here .. beneath the
starry night.

Find every star my love .. and count them one by
one.
Go ahead and try .. and when you think you're
done ..

A billion more were born up there .. just out of
sight ..
The light from them someday .. another starry
night.

And so my love .. gaze deep up there into the
starry sea.
At all the fires burning there .. and then come
back to me.
And I will tell you how my love it shines as
bright ..
And burns as hot as any star up there .. in the
starry night.

I knew this woman once and she wanted to see
the stars through a telescope .. so I bought her
one.

Poem .. 20

Eternal Lonesome

How far is far enough until I say no more.
To find that place where I belong.
Where over that last hill I hope is home.
But finding that its not! That hope is wrong!
But on I go .. down a road that stretches
On and on the end unknown how far I from.
Just me alone there followed by..
That dam old ache inside .. eternal lonesome.

So on I go .. searching for the place
A place where I belong .. that I fit in ..
Stubbornly head bent down straight on.
Step by step against the odds into the wind ..
Searching for the place I hope to find one day.
In the valley there below and cry .. home!
And pray .. it will ease inside of me the pain ..
That damning ache inside ..
Eternal Lonesome.

I have always had that damn ache inside my
heart. I suppose I always will.

Poem .. 21

For all the Philip Nolans and the skies of home
they never saw again.

Gone Forever Skies

I watched the Sun set
Sinking slow into the sea.
It was as beautiful as anything ..
ever seen by me.

I saw twilight turn to night
and stars begin to shine.
A sign an endless circle ..
light and fire never dies.

On deck with aching heart
I closed these eyes of mine.
I saw home and the dying sun
in gone forever skies.

I watched the rays proclaim
the coming of the light.
A stunning sight the rising sun
and the dying of the night.

For dark gives way to light

and shining stars are gone.
Then day is born and now
its turn .. the darkness dies.

And everywhere as fire spreads
consuming gentle dawn ..
I see home and the rising sun ..
in gone forever Skies.

Philip Nolan was the main Factious character in
the book "The Man without a Country" by
Edward Everett Hale. A young man who was
condemned to never see his country again. Read
this book .. or watch the movie .. and you will
know from where this poem was born.

Poem .. 22

Fear

He'll scream in you to run ..
When its time to make a stand.
He'll freeze your every muscle ..
In times you should have ran.

He'll steal from you control ..
Then come pouring out your skin.
He'll fight you every second ..
To be master there within.

He'll make you tremble ..
When your trying to be still.
He'll have you talking loud ..
Pretending courage never real.

He'll squeeze you by the throat ..
And you won't talk at all.
With each brave step you take ..
He'll laugh your going to fall.

He'll say you'll never win ..
Long before the fight begins.
When your heart is broke ..
He'll say .. never love again.

Brave the dark unknown .. and he'll
Cry into the darkness .. never go.
Try to show your gentle side ..
He'll cry don't ever show.

Faced with Death he'll make
You beg to God and whimper to.
He'll make you cry .. forgive me.
Knowing no one .. is forgiving you.

He'll even make you pray ..
When you've never prayed before.
He'll crawl inside your heart ..
And there he'll be ... FEAR forever more.

Have you ever been afraid? I mean really afraid.
I   have

Poem .. 23

The Why

Yang is white the sun and light.
Yin is black the moon and night.
He is yang and she is yin.
No matter why .. just two of them.

Black is here because of white.
It is dark to light and day to night.
White is here because of black ..
And both are balanced back to back.

For every good their is the bad.
One joyful tear .. one tear so sad.
For every wrong there is one right ..
as they spin they love and fight.

At every end there is beginning.
Some are not and some are singing.
Next to silence their is sound.
In harmony a balance there is found.

Their is to close and way to far apart.
In both a piece of the other's heart.
For every low their comes a high.
And Yin and Yang they are the why.

Yin and yang is about balance in the universe ..
and in your life and heart. Look it up .. and you
will understand where this poem was born.

Poem .. 24

Holy Ground

For all of us there is a door.
Behind where peace is sought ..
In many names on blessed floor.
In temples or in silent forest found ..
For each our own we seek ..
This place we call .. our holy ground.

But in some of us a war is fought.
Where deep inside the hate it rages ..
How our faith is right .. all others not.
So peace is burned and bugles sound ..
As that ugly human part it rises up ..
And blood is shed on Holy ground.

But in-between the Gods and all alone ..
There stands this poet heart afire.
All faith he guards as each his own ..
By pen or sword he's honor bound.
By one or the other .. to safely keep ..
For each his own .. his Holy ground.

Everyone of us has that special place we call our
Holy ground. I strongly believe this and respect

each one his or her holy ground. And so should
you.

Poem .. 25

Losing

Grieving by the grave you realize ..
For words unsaid there is .. no excusing.
For all your scars cut deep inside ..
Every one was carved by losing.

Stomped and beaten to the ground ..
In defeat there broke and bruising.
You lay in tears of rage and realize ..
There is no pain compared to Losing.

The thief of love he comes and goes.
He steals your heart .. your love refusing.
Too late you find he has no heart.
Except of course .. the one your Losing.

Life is war and every day a battle.
Fighting back.. against the taking and the using.
But never forget .. that courage is born ..
or courage dies .. in the fire of losing.

When you fall you have two choices .. get up …
or   lay   there.

Poem .. 26

Spiraling Down In Flame's

All my life I've spent to find
True love .. before I died.
But how I burned my life to bone ..
To find but this .. true love she lied.

So one false lover and then another ..
I am haunted by the names.
I the unforgiven .. for never bending ..
Spiraling down in Flame's.

Never bending ... will be the death of us all.

Poem .. 27

The Black Sheep

Give me the ones who don't fit in.
For whom that die we never weep.
The ones outside the bleating flock ..
The ones they call ... the black sheep.

Give me the ones the Warrior ones.
Whose river runs so calm and deep.
The rebellious ones with heart's afire.
The ones they call .. the black sheep.

Give me the ones who walk the talk.
The defiant ones are those I'll keep ..
The ones they stamped no good I want ..
The ones they call .. the black sheep.

Give me the ones the lonely ones ..
Whose tears are buried deep.
Give me the ones who shun the herd.
The ones they call .. the black sheep.

I have always shunned the herd. I stamped my
self no good .. but by God .. I walked the talk.
We   all   should   walk   the   talk.

Poem .. 28

The Angel of No Mercy

He is the spirit of vengeance.
And the servant of all holy.
He is the master of violence.
The angel of no mercy.

On his banner emblazoned.
His name by the God all mighty.
Carved by fire into his sword.
The Angel of no Mercy.

On his forehead burned across ...
The Angel of no Mercy.
Close behind him follows Hell.
He is death .. the sacred prophecy.

As the bugles blow .. Degüello.
On a pale horse comes no pity.
The tempest howls in rage it cries ..
Behold .. the Angel of no Mercy.

This poem was born from the 1611 King James
Bible, Revelations 6:7-8. Check it out. Except I
kind of changed it a little bit. You might be

thinking .. what the heck does The word degüello mean? Well it signifies the act of beheading or throat-cutting and in Spanish history became associated with battle music, which, in different versions, meant complete destruction of the enemy.........without mercy. If you know the history of what happened at the Alamo in 1836 ... you will understand the word.

Poem .. 29

Between The Dark And The Light

One foot in the dark and one in the light.
Despair to the left and hope to the right.
Drawn to the one side and then to the other ..
From the first breath .. till never another.
Where the one side is wrong and the other right.
One foot in the dark .. and one in the light.

Well .. we all walk this line as we wobble down
the road of life. All of us stray into the dark at
one point or another .. Lets all hope and pray we
find   the   light.

Poem .. 30

The Big Bang

By their calculations .. many a billion years ago.
Wise men said the world was born .. they know.
But in their calculations .. please they say excuse
..
One fact we can not figure .. who lit the fuse.

Now just by common sense.. a long long time
ago.
I an ignorant man .. the world was born I know.
But I think that day my God he had the blues.
And said .. ah hell .. what a mess and lit the fuse.

As good a theory as anyone else's Right?

Poem .. 31

A Poem For an Atheist

Soon in blessed peace I'll sleep.
No nightlight in the darkest deep.
No pain no sorrow no guilty heart.
Just fast asleep in the deepest dark.

Until the darkness comes I'll wait.
When from life to death I'll graduate.
No heaven nor hell when I depart.
Just fast asleep .. in the deepest dark.

I do not know what I believe comes after death.
But I sure know what I want to believe.

Poem .. 32

<u>Sins</u>

For every sin you think what's done is done?
Well I know its not they'll haunt you every one.
You'd better grit your teeth to stand the ache.
For Pain is coming .. for every sin you make.

Did you know some sins there's no forgiving?
Like every soul you choked and starved.
And I've heard somewhere beyond the living ..
You will pay for every notch you carved.

As Clint Eastwood said in his 1992 western movie "We all got it coming kid"

Drums

I do not understand inside the pounding.
Why I hear the sound of beating drums.
How I feel the beat of freedom sounding.
And raging from my heart the fire comes.

I feel upon my face the paint of war.
As I'm dancing to the pounding drums.
In a vision I'm an eagle and high above I soar.
And raging from my heart the fire comes.

I do not understand inside the pounding.
My skin is white .. yet still I hear the drums.
But then I hear a distant bugle sounding.
And raging from my heart the fire comes.

Did you ever see the movie Little Big Man? This
Poem was born from watching that movie ..
And my cousin Rick always said ... David .. I
think you have Indian blood in you.
I   think   we   all   do.

Poem .. 34

The Littleness of I

In a mighty deafening crash ..
Lightning burned through sky.
In a jagged streaking flash ..
Exposed I stood .. the littleness of I.

In my circle safe within ..
I watched above the raging sky.
From light to dark and back again ..
Defiantly I stood .. the littleness of I.

When you gaze out into the stars its really easy
to know .. if you have any sense ... just how
little we are. But we all get a little defiant now
and then. But our time is coming.

Poem .. 35

For my Father
The battle of Iwo Jima February 19, 1945 ..
World War II

Black Sand

Carve these words in stone I said.
To die in battle may be better than to not.
For peace comes quickly for the dead ..
But the living with dark dreams in hand ..
Fear to sleep .. for fear to crawl again ..
Through blood and death .. and black sand..

My Father was a US Marine in World Two and was in the battle too take Iwo Jima from the Japanese. He had nightmares for years about this battle and told me in detail about his dreams and his time on Iwo. And so this is where this poem was born. God rest his soul.

Poem .. 36

In The Shadow Of Your Brain

Your way is the only way ..
Everyday the same old whine.
I can even hear you singing ..
How my little light does shine.

Your head blocks out the sun.
I watch you wallow in the light.
While in the shadow of your brain ..
I cling to sanity .. with all my might.

I knew this guy at work once …. Ah never mind
.. we all have known someone with a big head.

Poem .. 37

I have Cried

I have cried in rage .. I have cried in pain.
I have cried in sadness .. I have cried in rain.
I have cried alone and I have cried goodbye.
I have cried for beauty .. never wondering why.

I have cried for others .. when others I saw cry.
I have cried for nothing always wondering why.
I have cried inside .. deep where none could see.
I have cried for love .. and love has cried for me.

We have all cried for one reason or another. If
you have never cried .. you are a stone and rock
hard.

Poem ..38

The Knot

Will you take this woman..
To bare her sadness and pains.
Do you promise to cover her..
If the sun burns or the sky rains.

Will you take this woman..
As an equal and a best friend..
Do you promise to stand by her..
And in thy stubbornness bend.

Will you take this woman..
To be loyal thru day and night ..
Until you die .. and if beyond ..
Even in the dark or the light.

Do you take this woman ..
Promising she'll never ask of you ..
Not once .. Do you love me?
Cause one touch will say you do.

Do you take this woman ..
And with her pull tight the knot.
Knowing if undone or ever cut.
Love will die .. and forever be forgot.

A friend of mine was getting married and ask me to write a poem he could read to his bride that day. I told him it takes me months to write one poem. He said .. please try. So I did and he read this poem to his bride.

Handfasting - The Irish .. Tie the Knot .. Hand fasting is an ancient Celtic custom in which a man and woman came together at the start of their marriage. Their hands, or more accurately, their wrists were literally tied together. This practice gave way to the expression "tying the knot". One legend believes the Celtic Knot means eternal love because it has no beginning and no end. Thus the belief if the knot is undone in any way true love will die.

Poem .. 39

There is a Reason and a Rhyme.

For every thing that dies.
For true love once in one life time.
For every sundown and sunrise.
There is a reason and a rhyme.

For every wrong done.
And all tears shed in one lifetime.
For stars shinning .. every one.
There is a reason and a rhyme.

.

For every hope lost .. and then found.
Why the dark runs from the sunshine.
For Earth spinning slowly round.
There is a reason or rhyme.

.

For every step that's taken.
Up every mountain that we climb.
For the chosen and the Godforsaken.
There is a reason and a rhyme.

I believe that there is a reason for every little
thing that happens in our lives .. where we go ..

why we go .. even who we bump into while
stumbling down the road of life.

Poem .. 40

You Have Never Dreamed

If you have never on the highest rock ..
Trembling there .. in triumph screamed.
For suffering the climb .. the long hard walk.
Then you have never dreamed.

If you have never felt inside the pain ..
Of defeat .. complete and unredeemed.
Like a fire drowned by the cold rain.
Then you have never dreamed.

If you have passed the unattainable ..
Just for the impossible .. that it seemed.
Then you have never done the unbelievable.
And you sir .. have never dreamed.

Never .. Never .. give up on your dreams .. if you
do you will hate yourself when your old and on
your   dying   bed.

Poem .. 41

When Will Jesus Come

In Benghazi Americans died there...
While the man was sucking his thumb.
In our land .. holy wars are everywhere.
And I wonder .. when will Jesus come.

The lambs in the dark they pray for dawn.
While hyenas on two legs yap and run.
Were like stray dogs by the road abandoned ..
And I wonder .. when will Jesus come.

Distant sirens crying .. in the cold night air.
Out in the streets the killings are .. never done.
In the back of my pants .. I feel my 45 there.
And I wonder .. when will Jesus come.

We live in troubled times and there are some
who wish to disarm us .. I think not.

Poem .. 42

Where Poems Are Born

If you take the path on through the eyes.
And follow it down winding through the heart.
Then down into the soul where the spirit lies ..
Past hope falling down .. into the deepest part.

There at the bottom is a dark and empty space ..
Where old memories lie all broke and torn.
And there among .. the silent sadness of the
place.
You will have found .. where poems are born.

Poems can be born in dark places or born in the
shinning   light.

Poem .. 43

Lucifer

He gazed up into the star lit night .. and spit.
Preparing for battle .. caring not it was written.
His destiny by Gods decree .. to burn forever ..
The angel of betrayal .. Lucifer the unforgiven.

In the valley of Armageddon .. he waited there.
The king of hell full of hate and defiance.
A rebel fallen angel .. haunted by the words ..
Lucifer I am coming .. I who loved you once.

Lucifer 's army and Gods army. It takes place in
the valley of Armageddon a real place in Israel.
Lucifer's army of course is defeated. This is my
vision of Lucifer waiting at Armageddon
impatiently for God to attack. And remember
God once loved Lucifer above all others. Though
Lucifer knows he will be defeated he will not
accept the thought of it.

Poem .. 44

There by the Sea

If you can hear me guide her there I softly
prayed.
Through the deserts on her journey far from me.
Guide her through the mountains and the valleys.
To her sacred place grant her peace there by the
sea.

If I beg upon my knees .. could you I humbly
ask.
Walk beside her on the beach .. one more time
for me.
If your up there God like she believes .. for this I
pray..
Bring her safely home .. heart healed there by
the sea.

I knew this girl once and we were a couple but I
thought that it was not working and so we broke
up because that is what I wanted. She took off to
her favorite place by the ocean and I wrote this
poem. Remember .. sometimes when your young
.. you think your immortal and you do stupid
things,   God   forgive   me.

Poem .. 45

In Honor of all U.S. Veterans

I Never Was a Soldier

I never was a soldier and I never will be one.
But o'er the fallen .. this bugle call I know.
The call that stills the breath and echo's cross ..
Far away graves .. in fields where poppies grow.

I never was a soldier but my father he was one.
And in his eyes I saw reflections of his war.
I never held the hand .. of my comrade dying.
But I in honor rise .. when filing by ..
Go the Warrior corps.

My war was the Vietnam war .. every generation
has one ... but I never went to mine. I was
married at 19 and my new bride was with child ..
They gave me a 3A draft deferment because of
it. I was happy at the time but every day since I
have been so ashamed of my self and will be to
the   day   I   die.

Poem .. 46

Creation

He never made the whale ..
until he made the sea ..
For them to swim in.

He never made the eagle
until he made the sky ..
for them to fly in.

He never made forever ..
until he made the gold ..
To pave the streets of heaven in.

He never made the truth ..
until he made the lie ..
For us to wallow in.

He never made the fear ..
until he made the hell ..
To throw us in.

He never made the man ..
until he made the evil ..
to put inside of him.

Not really sure what brought these words on ..
Just another twisted version of creation.

Poem .. 47

Run Little Pony Run

In the shimmering distance ..
Straight out of the sun.
Came a horse and a rider ..
Run little pony run.

Through the tall grass waving ..
Pony bucking just for fun.
Past old bones in wild places ..
Run little pony run.

To the mountains blue beyond ..
Straight to the far horizon.
Past prairie dogs and buffalo ..
Run little pony run.

Like the wind across the plains ..
Race horse and man as one.
Through the night and the rain ..
Run little pony run.

Two hearts big and pounding.
Until the singing wire is done.
For eighteen months of glory ..
Run little pony run.

The Pony Express

In April 1860, the Pony Express began to deliver the mail from Saint Joseph, Missouri, to Sacramento, California. The mail was then taken by boat to San Francisco. Relays of young, lightweight, riders covered the 3,164-km (1,966-mi) journey in about 10 days. These riders faced hazardous weather conditions and some very unhappy Native Americans. The Pony Express closed in October 1861, when the telegraph lines were completed. The Native Americans called them .. the singing wires.

Poem .. 48

Blessed Be The Sound

Black boots and a Harley ..
Stomp that crank goodbye.
Across my leather written ..
A hog riding Samurai.

I lean her hard to port.
Two lane curving round.
Jacket all zipped up ..
Blacktop rumbling down.

Shades as black as night.
Hair blowing in the wind.
My wild heart calling ..
For places never been.

Throaty roar sweet music ..
Hard kick her out of town.
Like trumpets blowing charge ..
Blessed be the sound.

If you have ever rode a motorcycle .. especially a
Harley ..

Then you know what I was writing about and
where   this   poem   was   born.

Poem .. 49

Monsoon

Low above the desert floor.
Black clouds are on the way.
Bulging belly's full of rain ..
Just another monsoon day.

Lightning flashing all around.
Zig zagging cross the sky.
Thirsty dirt holds up her cup ..
Waiting for the clouds to cry.

Ancient rivers born a new.
As water falls and water flows.
Big ole rain drops falling down ..
As the monsoon comes and goes.

I can smell the desert rain.
And the slamming of heavens doors.
Its natures dance .. a wild ballet ..
Giving life and taking its what she knows.

Watch her dancing lighting show.
Hear her grumbling up above.
Feel the fury of her rage ..
But oh my God ..

These monsoon days .. I love.

If you have ever experienced Monsoon season in Southern Arizona USA ... you will understand this   poem.

Poem .. 50

She Dances in Her Heart

I WHO WALK
Looked down and saw her there ..
All beautifully alone.
I heard them whispering .. ear to ear ..
Her legs are dead .. as dead as stone.
But her head was high her eyes intent ..
On what she knew .. she'd never be a part.
Then her gaze met mine .. I smiled ..
She knew I knew .. She dances in her heart.

I WHO WALK
Kneeled down before her whispering ..
May I have this dance with you?
Before her giggly no I swept her from
Her chair .. and round the room we flew.
I danced on legs of strength .. she danced
On air .. her feet and floor this far apart.
And with her arms around my neck .. I smiled.
She knew I knew .. She dances in her heart.

I WHO WALK
I the coward .. who runs from love ..
If ever love would come to near.

But I Danced with she .. who couldn't walk ..
Who clung to me in faith .. not fear.
I sat her gently down .. her smile it lit the night.
Then her soul .. so quickly did depart.
Her in my arms .. I Cried not yet! .. but knew ..
The dancing died inside her heart.

I WHO WALK
Kneeled with flowers setting them ..
Each one just right about her grave.
I pondered just how precious .. is this life ..
If God to her .. so precious little gave.
I cried as always .. why not me? .. as I read ..
The words there carved in stone .. the part
That said where ever she may be ..
She dances now on legs of strength .. I smiled ..
She knew I knew .. She dances in her heart.

This poem was born from a dream I had ... I
woke up .. jumped up .. and started writing.

Poem .. 51

For Sara

To Never Be Forgotten

To never be forgotten as first love's not
forgotten.
Nor the heart so broken when first love dies.
Let it never be forgotten for ever and ever ...
Her words of fire singing ... all their sad
goodbyes.

If anyone should ask .. say .. let it never be
forgotten.
Like a flower saved .. between the pages .. long
ago ..
Let it never be forgotten .. for ever and ever ...
Her sad words gently calling .. soft as falling
snow.

I wrote this poem in response to the poem
written by Sara Teasdale ..Let It Be Forgotten
She is .. and always will be .. my most favorite
poet.

Made in the USA
Columbia, SC
22 May 2023

17159509R00046

Michelle Ruddell

Trust in him at all times, you people;
pour out your hearts to him,
for God is our refuge.
Psalm 62: 5-8